Proof That I Have A Heart

Calcifer Benitex

BookLeaf Publishing

India | USA | UK

Presentation by *BookLeaf Publishing*

Web: www.bookleafpub.com

E-mail: info@bookleafpub.com

ISBN: 9789360944100

First edition 2024

ACKNOWLEDGEMENT

Chloe, you will always be famous for braving my continuous batches of poems and stories filled with my weeping. Thank you for your bravery.

i. First Love

She is the first,
Opened my eyes to the world
And sings me to sleep.
Captivated by this childlike grip
On my young heart,
I cling to her lapels.
To that wonderful girl,
You are the first.

ii. First Goodbye

Distant memory,
The first can only be that.
Goodnight, ghostly girl.

i. In this one

You and I lay upon a bed, connected by a phone
wire like two pinkies curled together.
Even at the end of the world, we would remain
tethered.

You often wonder why you are unloved, and I
hold my tongue to keep my adoration from
spilling at your feet.
I pray for a day when your clever gaze no longer
makes me retreat.

No one can compare to your beauty and wit; no
one knows my heartbeat as well as you.
Is it presumptuous of me to believe that you feel
the same, too?

You play tricks and hold contempt for many, but
for me, you are fond; how special it is that I'm
shown your grace.
We promise to live together, but can two
opposing forces exist in the same space?

Your delicate hands reach for mine, but we are at
an impasse.

Perhaps we were soulmates before, but here, our time has run out on the hourglass.

ii. In another

In another life, you're sitting on your favorite
spot on the couch, legs crossed, and crocheting a
sweater. Sunlight streams through the curtains in
ribbons, framing your face like a gift. I'm
standing in the doorway in my favorite shoes
and thinking: I will happily drown in this bliss.

i. Stolen Secrets

Your eyes are like toffee, sickeningly sweet.
Sitting beside you, I am jittery.
Do I look like a newborn foal stumbling in your
direction?

You try so hard to impress me, but it's not me
you're seeing.
I exist behind a carefully constructed persona; I
am not who I say I am.

I keep my lies under lock and key.
They pile up one by one with a quickening pace
until I am caught underneath the weight of them.

I look into your toffee eyes and see the future
you envision with me,
but it's not me.
It's that dastardly other I've constructed, the
thing I hide behind.

There's a lovely bouquet on my doorstep.
It might be possible, it could be true.
I open up to the fresh air to see you
standing with that cheeky smile.
Clumsily, I return the favor

and tell you who I am.

Isn't it so funny?
The flowers start to rot on the concrete.

ii. Stolen Truths

I know you're out there
Among the cliff-sides by the ocean.
My truth overwhelmed you, so you escaped.
I can't say I blame you.

I am a carcass; you, a vulture. With my viscera
in your mouth, do you enjoy stringing it across
the canyons?

I'm sure I've become a rather disgusting
memory. What was your expression like when
you turned away from me on my doorstep?
Twisted and broken? Wrathful and confused?

Only a week passed until you were arm-in-arm
with another. You kissed them goodbye on their
doorstep; those flowers are practically dust on
mine.

I am a fool to believe anything other than the
truth. I belong in the shadows, forced to look
from the outside in.

I press against the glass to watch you abandon
me. I doubt you can hear my anguish.

i. Bluebeard

You exist in a foggy haze, obscured by the lies
you tell.

Summer settles her warm blanket upon us, legs
intertwined.

Your blind followers come clamoring at the
sound of your bell.

I ask you to treat me kindly, but your eyes drown
in molasses—it's time for you to raise hell.

You whisper goodnight; I sink underneath that
awful moon, resigned.

I will always wonder if you felt betrayed as well.

ii. His Seventh Wife

Obsessed, you say! What a clever little joke
from the cult leader himself. Tell me, how does
it feel to be the messiah of the narcissists?

Perhaps I'm another left in your massacre across
the city, but aren't I so memorable? I had a
million and one fingers pointing your way.

I may have been ostracized, but all your puppets
clamored at your feet, desperate for the attention
I allegedly stole.

Your charisma is all you have going for you;
you're rotten to the core. One of these days,
worms might just crawl out of your orifices. I'll
laugh when the day comes.

I suppose I should count myself lucky; I
survived. You still have so many brainwashed
puppies trotting in your shadow.

I cared for you openly, pledged an allegiance
that only I can grant. But how odd, you cared in
silence. We sat in the catacombs of your heart. I

know you intended for me to die there like the
rest, but I'm too clever, just like you.

The memory of my betrayal weighs like
dumbbells on your legs, dragging you deeper
into your deceit.

Send me a postcard from hell, darling.

i. Lapdog, Lemming, Sheep, That's me

According to you, I am fascinating.

Warnings blare in the background, but they blur
into a warm puddle at my feet. I'm overcome
with a flush of red; such praise is foreign.

Like always, you answer me in the dead of
night. Imposing and tall, I feel cornered. I feel
like a deer lost in your headlights.

You slaughter me with your saccharine flattery,
and I lap it up; distantly, I wonder if this is worth
it. I'm swept away again; your arms encase me
while your timber voice says I'm pretty again.

You murmur that there's no one like me, but you
choose everyone except me. I teeter on the edge
of insanity by your non-commitment.

We meet in a coffee shop; a beautiful scent
circles me—a false sense of security. Stay with
me, I plead. I am no longer there with you; your
eyes are glass, and to you, I'm an obstacle. I

perch myself on your back, and you keep me
there. For what, who knows?

I tell myself that I live in your heart.
Surely, I'll be enough one day.

ii. Vampire, Mosquito, Leech, You name it

There it is again, that knock on my window.
Your voice is like a rusty pipe snapping in two.
Hands snake around my waist; I feel sick, yet I
fall into your arms, caged like a featherless bird.

I keep letting you in, my deplorable vampire. I
wonder which will run out first: your need to
siphon my attention or my desire to keep you
fed.

Each time you appear, you look worse than
before—a walking corpse. I am too weak to bury
you, overcome with the false hope that you'll
finally choose me.

Ignore me, insult me, lavish me with your
self-inflicted issues. It's always rinse and repeat.

I know that in your eyes, I am beneath you, an
insignificant insect you keep in a jar to poke and
irritate. I should bite you, poison you, curse you.

Still, I'm too soft for the likes of you. My last
drop of blood comes in the form of silence.

So stop looking for me. I am no longer the fool
you hope me to be.

i. caring for a wren

maybe i'm in love,
perhaps the heaviness in my chest
is no longer the weight of an empty heart.

i want to hold you, softly and tightly,
just to remind myself that you're there.
i want to dance, holding your hand in mine,
as we swing around a cramped dorm room.

i want to fold your laundry,
keep you healthy,
bring you food,
sew your torn sleeves.

i cried in bed last night,
gratefulness rising up like bile in my throat.
i read about a man who found love,
even after he was abandoned.
i am no longer discarded trash,
no broken glass.

i want to sink into your ocean,
let the water absorb me until i'm sea foam.
i want to lift you towards the sun
because you shine brighter than any star,

and all i am is icarus,
flying toward you despite the risk.

can you keep me warm
and keep me whole?
can you love me until i'm nothing more than a
floating soul?
i'll stay with you until kingdom come,
so maybe i am in love.

ii. THE WREN FLEW AWAY

WITH YOU,
I PRETEND THAT I AM LOVED.
YOU ARE THE OCEAN I FALL INTO: SOFT,
SOFT, SOFT.
WHEN YOUR ARMS OF BRITTLE CAGE
ME,
I FEEL LIKE SYRUP SLIPPING THROUGH
THE CRACKS.
I KNOW YOU DON'T LOVE ME THE WAY I
LOVE YOU;
YOUR SILENCE DEALS THE HARDEST
PUNCHES.
MY HANDS COVER MY MOUTH UNTIL
MY CHEEKS BLEED,
AND I LAY ON THE FLOOR, BEGGING FOR
YOU TO LOOK AT ME.
MY SWEET ANGEL, WILL YOU PITY ME
JUST THIS ONCE?
I WANT TO FEEL WHOLE; I WANT TO BE
LOVED.
I SMILE AT YOU AS I PUSH MYSELF OFF
THE CLIFF I DANGLE OVER.
AT MY FUNERAL, WILL YOU SING FOR
ME?

WILL YOU SING AS MY LOVED ONES
WEEP ONTO MY CORPSE, AND WILL YOU
SING AS MY SPIRIT CARESSES YOUR
BEATING HEART?
I HOPE YOU CAN SLEEP PEACEFULLY
WITH YOUR NEWEST OBSESSION AS MY
RAGE SHAKES YOUR BED, SCREAMING
FOR YOU TO CALL MY NAME.
BUT I AM LOST TO THE WIND; YOU
FORGOT ABOUT ME SO EASILY.

IN DEATH, IT ALL BECOMES NULL.
I SUPPOSE THERE IS NOTHING LEFT TO
SAY.

i. How Sweet

It's rather nice to be loved;
I'd like to get used to it.

Would you be Hades, and I'll be your
Persephone?
Yes,
It's a tried and true love story.
Quite a tale for the modern day.

Do you see us in the past or future, my dear?
I imagine us in the present.
I'm a coward, you see.
I want to last for as long as human lives go.
But flowers wilt too fast,
And I can't bear to face such a reality.

Will you stay with me as I gingerly eat a
pomegranate?
We can share the seeds as lovers do.

It's rather nice to love;
Can you get used to it?

ii. How Bitter

Your love is pure and decadent,
While I am convinced that something grotesque
is slithering around me.
Convinced this was it, you made your bed,
But I will start packing my luggage after you fall
asleep.

You pull us forward to a nest you built for me;
I can't bring myself to cross the threshold.
You tell me I'm the only one,
But I'll never be the right one.

You dream of our wedding bells;
I hear the knell reverberate through my body.
Joy wraps itself around you when you see me,
And I watch the grief consume you when I
leave.

I'm so sorry we weren't the ones to cross that
finish line.
I'll stand in the background, cheering, when I
watch you break the ribbon with your true love.

i. Purgatory or something

Words escape me, always with you.
They become cluttered and large in my mouth.
I consistently vomit them on you, full of fear
and nervousness and pure love.

I love you—it feels like a blessing.
I almost wrote down a curse, but loving you was
a privilege.
When you spun and dipped me in your living
room, it felt better than any professional dancer
could do.
Your fleeting kisses against my cheeks,
forehead, lips—how heavenly they felt.
Your arms around me while we slept, my dear, I
knew nothing could hurt me.

You are such a sweet soul.
I remember on our last night, you asked me to
hug you. It was the first thing you've ever asked
of me.
We laid side by side, and I held you all night.
I hoped we would never wake up, but morning
came,
as it always does.

I am brittle; I am shattered.
I am selfish, so I pray that I stay with you
forever.
Please, see me in your dreams and feel my touch
in your memories.

I am unsure of how to move on; I do not want to
move on.
The idea of brushing against another's fingertips
is almost revolting.
It is wrong; it feels like a betrayal.
I love you with all my heart; how could I do
anything differently?

I am tired of another world; I want it to be this
one.
I want you to be with me, here, in my bed.
I want to kiss you in public, and meet your
parents, and move in with you.
I want all those unfortunate cliches.

I can never say this to you.
there is a wall you put up that I cannot break
down, but my love,
I am on the other side, waiting.

ii. Deliverance maybe

It's over. There's no attractive way to spin it, no yarn that would make the descent easier. The realization is violent, as dangerous as a body slamming onto kitchen tiles, dry heaving. My tongue sits heavy in my drooling mouth, and my eyes threaten to pop out of my sockets. It's over, I repeat. It's over, it's over!

I sleep on the floor that night, illuminated by the streetlight sitting outside my window—no moon drooping above me, no stars twinkling its sorrow. I cackle, wondering what entity had pieced this malfunctioning body together. Truly, my love could not be love. My love was a bastardized version of everyone else's, a mere mockery of the word even. I could find no beauty in such a feeling. Swirling within me was a terrifying guilt, a monster too giant for its crumbling shell.

I tremble under this frightening husk and, for a moment, wish I had less respect for myself. Should I claw down your door or snarl at your steps inching away from me? My instinct is desperation, a heart so distorted that it struggles

to discern affection from despair. I am an
amalgamation of obsession and desire. If I
could, I'd eat you whole and savor every bite.
Then, it'd never be over, right?

But, another tremor washes through, and I know
I must have more respect for myself. Begging
means little to a stranger; I am nothing more
than a whimpering dog in a damp alleyway. If
it's over, I must lick my wounds and limp back
to the spot in the grass where the sun shines
brightest. Behind the infatuation, I am also
sensible and tender. Hunger will return, and the
reality is that you are still gone. It's always over,
isn't it?

With a deep breath, I must bid you a kiss
goodbye. The dew will settle, and the clouds
will meander; a new day is coming. It may not
be romantic, it may not be beautiful, but it's
over, and I have no regrets.

i. Angels & Redwood

Astigmatism makes the lights on the road flash
so very bright, almost like an angel is trying to
send a message. I'm not a religious man; I
suppose the prophecy is lost on me.

My father drives through those blinding stars
and, without looking at me, says:

"To deal with the grief they give you, go out to
the garden and dig a hole. When you're ready,
bury it. Until then, I'll cry with you."

I watch as flowers bloom from the soil in my
backyard. Forget-me-nots scattered like a
graveyard. Maybe it is. My salty tears
continuously nourish the petals. My father pats
me on the back. "I'm sorry you're in pain," he
whispers.

After every wound, I come home to see his
outline standing at the edge of our driveway. My
lungs constrict; at least, I know I have him.

We walk arm and arm; I tell him I might die
alone. He nods solemnly. "It'll happen one day.

Someone will appear." I duck under the weight
of his assuredness, tears pricking once again at
my corners. His faith in me is unparalleled. I
hope I can live up to it.

I ask the stars to keep him by my side. I wish
with every atom inside that he lives long enough
to see me hand in hand with a lovely soul. He
deserves to see me at my purest, love brimming
around me like a halo.

I can't predict the strings of fate, but even then,
if some tragedy were to slip into our lives, I
promised I would take him to see the redwood
trees.

Among the towering gods, I'll tell him that
someone finally showed up.

i. Everlasting

My dearests,

It's been twenty-four hours and a year since I've
last seen you. Do you dream of me when salt is
thick in the air? The water beckons us back so
we can play like the children we could never be.

I remember the ratty chairs and stiff couches we
draped ourselves across.
We lay like newborn kittens piled across their
mother and watched our favorite things.

I wait for you like a soldier's wife.
Leaning against the doorframe, there might
come a day when I see your car pull into my
driveway. I'll nestle into your heart, knowing
there will never be a day where I run cold.

We'll weep in each other's arms over the past
and frolic among the seeds of the future. If
there's anyone to look forward to living a life
with, it's you.

Promise you'll stay; you feel like home.

i. To You

There's a little girl whose vacant eyes follow me
as my ankles bend and twist in the fog.
I shudder to imagine what she could possibly
think of me, what I've grown up to be.

All I am is a blasphemous man who prays to
false gods, hoping one of them will be stupid
enough to bestow their grace unto me.
And yet,
deep down, so deep that it reaches where this
little girl lives, I know that the only angel
watching over me
is
me?

It's me. It's her. It's him. It's still me.
It was me who clawed my chest open to reveal
my stitched heart, and it was me who sent those
final kisses.
It was me who closed the door, and it was me
who cradled my crushed soul.
My naivety is my grief is my scorn is my
tenderness is my love.

Despite the humiliation, despite the loss, despite
it all, does the little girl hold pride for me?
With each rainfall, does the monster that
entombs me wash away? Does she see me?

All I am is just me. Just me with a twisted heart
too big for my body,
but it's me nonetheless.

ii. to me

and she says,
"everyone you've ever shared your heart with is
mere paper. your love to them is a love letter to
yourself.
how capable you are, how soft, how sturdy.
there is no shame in following the strings that
promise you salvation.
ever so slowly, you learn.
i am stuck in a moment in time, forbidden to
move forward or back,
but you are a moving monolith,
extending your arms towards others despite the
sharp edges.

of course, i am proud. you are me, and i am you.

it's still you."